WHY IS THE GLOBAL ECONOMY LIKE THIS?

WHY IS THE GLOBAL ECONOMY LIKE THIS?

Cornelis Bal

PARTRIDGE
A Penguin Random House Company

Print information available on the last page.

To order additional copies of this book, contact
Toll Free 800 101 2657 (Singapore)
Toll Free 1 800 81 7340 (Malaysia)
orders.singapore@partridgepublishing.com

www.partridgepublishing.com/singapore

Contents

Preface

This book discusses:

- the way our global economy is structured

- how this structure rules our lives almost completely

- why we accept that structure

- suggestions for how the economy can be changed.

I've used common sense. The language is as simple as possible, making it understandable to everyone. I have refrained from using elaborate mathematical models to support my conclusions, as I feel that they will confuse the issue.

My father used to say, "You don't have to pick up dog shit to know that it stinks."

So instead, I use history to show how humankind has evolved and to predict the future.

Another person in my life who I wish to mention is my wife, Susan. She loves me, and I love her more than anything else in this world.

I also wish to thank all the authors, lecturers, and others from whom I have accumulated the wisdom expressed in this book.

Finally, I wish to thank Partridge for excellent editing.

Chapter 1

Introduction

This book is about the way in which our global society is organised. It identifies how this format came about.

It also shows that it can be changed.

Unlike the laws of nature, economic laws are man-made, so they can be changed.

The present economic system is based on the fact that money is generated in the commercial sector of the economy. This money, generated by individuals and corporations, is skimmed off by taxes. Governments use these taxes to cover their expenses, including support of the unemployed.

Although the economy is growing, the number of people and corporations involved in the money-generating process is shrinking. This means that the number of people depending on the people generating money will grow, leading to an imbalance.

The present economic system is supposed to increase freedom.

All of us like freedom. However, this is not the type of freedom that allows us to do whatever we want. Instead, it is freedom to do what we want within the constraints of a system, and we accept that. Even believers in total freedom stop at red traffic lights.

Have you ever wondered how much freedom is taken from us by the way our economic system is arranged?

The economic system rules our lives completely. It determines what we study, how we work (if we can get jobs), and how we raise our children.

The following old sayings directly affect us:

- Money is everything.

- If you are born to be a dime, you will never be a quarter (translated from Dutch).

- It is not affordable! (a very popular saying for governments)

The list of similar sayings is long.

The saying "We have to work for a living" indicates how important paying jobs are to us.

But does the present system create enough opportunities for us to do that?

To illustrate how the economic system is organised, I draw a comparison between two factors that rule our lives: the laws of nature and the law of economics.

The laws of nature lead us to build machines and use them. We build airplanes, motorcars, and ships, and we generate and use electricity. We live comfortably by using heating in cold countries and air-conditioning in hot countries. We can build high and sky-spanning structures. Most of us can swim, and that is probably one of best examples of using and enjoying the laws of nature. We can launch objects into outer space and keep them there. We can build computers and connect them with waves (in the form of Wi-Fi). We can watch television or listen to the radio. We can cure illnesses that were unknown a short time ago. We can even produce body parts for transplants. We can build weapons to hit people on the other side of the world without exposing ourselves. Some consider that very useful.

We apply the laws of nature to designing, building, and using many machines. The laws of nature are precise and dependable, and we should be grateful for them. There are still many unknown laws of nature. We call them mysteries, but they are not mysteries. We are simply not yet clever enough to have figured them out, or we have not yet fully worked out how multiple laws work together. Nature is beautiful.

- We can trust the laws of nature, as they are 100 per cent repetitive.

- The laws of nature also work over time as evolution.

- Figuring out the laws of nature helps us live longer and have easier lives.

- We learn how to use laws of nature at an increasing rate.

But we frequently take these laws for granted.

We do not always realise how helpless we would be if any of these laws stopped existing. It would be like the sun is switched off.

Discovery and use of the laws of nature follows an exponential curve. The difference between life fifty years ago and now is much more extreme than the difference between life five hundred years ago and fifty years ago.

If I had told my grandfather fifty years ago that I would be able to speak to somebody on the other side of the globe using a device as small as the package holding the tobacco that he used to roll his own cigarettes, he would have recommended that my father lock me up in an institution.

We couldn't predict what would happen in fifty years then, and we can't predict what will happen in *five* years now. Companies used to make yearly budgets and stick to them until the year was over. Companies now make rolling quarterly budgets, reviewing and adjusting them every three months. People once made long-term plans for twenty years in the future, but we now have difficulty reliably looking ahead two years.

The telex machine was around for one hundred years and peaked at 1.2 million machines in the world, and then it was replaced by the fax machine. There were 1.2 million fax machines operating within two years. But who uses fax machines now?

The life of technological products has been reduced to the point that they must prove profitable within two years of release or they're considered commercial failures.

Although there is basically nothing wrong with that pace, many of us (especially we older folks) are having difficulty coming to terms with the speed at which these developments are introduced. Another result is that schools have to educate students for jobs that don't exist yet.

The graph below depicts the pace of progress. Between five hundred years ago and fifty years ago, the line is almost horizontal, and between fifty years ago and today, it's almost vertical!

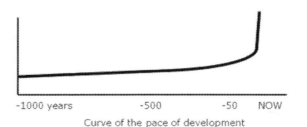

-1000 years   -500   -50   NOW

Curve of the pace of development

The rapid growth depicted by the almost vertical line does not seem to make us much smarter when it comes to managing our resources, however. For example, we take some resources from the environment much higher rates than those at which nature can replace them. We dig into our capital rather than living off the interest.

We do this when we use fossil fuels for generating energy.

We can generate plenty of energy from other sources, and we are capable of tapping those sources. We do not have an energy shortage; we just have no reliable means of storing energy. The best idea we have come up with so far is to put a small amount of energy into a battery.

The way we use energy can also be improved. Some people have estimated that 70 per cent of our energy is lost in transmission. Others have proven that trucks use up to 80 per cent of their fuel to power the truck and only 20 per cent to carry the load. We can move goods through pipelines much more cheaply and effectively than we do now. All this wastage has a negative impact on our environment.

Yes, *environment* and *nature* are my favourite words, and the "green" people are right in many ways, although they often fail to present their cases convincingly.

By nature, we accumulate knowledge over time. This is popularly known as *evolution*. For example, creeping plants "know" how to cling to other plants and climb towards the sun. Trees "know" to grow wide root systems to balance their heights.

In human civilization, the Chinese culture specifically recognises that present knowledge is inherited from ancestors and values ancient wisdom. This wisdom cannot always be scientifically proven. For example, modern Western medical science initially dismissed ancient Eastern medical wisdom, but it is increasingly recognised in the West as valuable because it is the evolved knowledge of millions of people over thousands of years.

So whatever brilliant idea we come up with is always thanks to the knowledge of other people before us. Even then, brilliance is often only recognised when it is a commercial success.

The laws of economics also have a major impact on our lives. They rule our thinking and planning. The laws of economics are not as predictable and reliable as the laws of nature, however. The economic laws have been created by a relatively small number of people who had and have both the power and selfish interest to create the rules and regulations as we now know them.

We seem to be stuck with these rules and regulations, and we are reluctant to even believe that we can change them.

In other words, the laws of nature apply to all people indiscriminately, while the laws of economics seem to favour only a limited number of people.

The first question I ask is this: why do we continue to accept current economic rules and regulations without question?

Chapter 2

The Laws of Economics

I want you to know that I am not a socialist; I am a realist!

The laws of economics focus on developing businesses so that people will benefit. However, this development has led to a concentration of money, leaving us with a world society that favours a limited number of people over all others.

Yes, this idea sounds socialistic, but as you read on, you'll see that it's realistic.

Our world has two basic economic systems: capitalism and communism. When the Soviet Union broke up and the influence of communism diminished in other countries, some people were of the opinion that capitalism had won.

It certainly seemed that way, but there are strong signs now that capitalism is about to fail too.

We cannot change the fact that humans operate from envy and greed, as if these characteristics were embedded in our DNA. These tendencies are definitely present in all of us, although they manifest themselves differently from individual to individual and from circumstance to circumstance.

The design parameters of any new system must include greed and envy otherwise it is bound to fail.

To understand how greed and envy affect our behaviour, consider this scenario: You're having dinner in a restaurant, and you happen to share a table with two strangers. Out of the blue, one stranger gives you a crisp, new one-hundred-dollar bill, no strings attached.

That makes you feel good, and you like that person. You have formed no particular opinion about the other person at the table yet.

Then the same stranger turns to the other guy and gives him two crisp one-hundred-dollar bills. Nobody took anything from you, but you no longer feel good, and you now have a peculiar feeling about the stranger who now has two hundred dollars. This is envy and greed working within you. You are ready to question the first stranger's actions even though he was generous to you.

All humans feel envy and greed, and as long as the actions they prompt do not harm our fellow human beings, they are very good at driving progress.

It is my opinion that communism tried to suppress these parts of human nature and replace them with a belief in a greater cause.

This does not work.

We are each unique, and we do not want to be considered equal to others.

We are proud of our achievements, and we want to be recognised and rewarded for them. We want to be *treated* equally, but that is different from *being* equal.

Capitalism recognises greed and envy and rewards them. It puts our greed and envy to good use by allowing them to drive progress. Capitalism works very well as long as we have fewer people than there are jobs but it works poorly when there are more people than jobs. Our economy is growing, but fewer and fewer people are involved in it. This is mainly a result of technological developments. As paid jobs disappear, joblessness increases, and this trend will continue. *This is a fact.*

Some people argue that manufacturing jobs are being replaced by service jobs. Those arguments are made mostly by people who produce robots. More and more things can be made by machines (robots); these machines can carry out service tasks too, and these machines are no longer limited only to hi-tech producers. Machines produce stuff and deliver services at increasingly low costs and high quality, and people's jobs disappear like snow in the sun. Hardly anyone processes your boarding pass or examines your passport to allow you to board an airplane. Instead:

- A machine reads your passport or a card and prints out your boarding pass.

- Another machine scans your fingerprint or your retina and allows you to pass immigration.

It is so much easier to get into any business producing products than it used to be, as machines have the skills to produce them and, soon, to replicate these skills in other machines. This accelerates jobs' shifting locations. What was traditionally an exclusively local product (Gouda cheese, Parma ham, etc.) can now be produced anywhere with machines. The owners of the machines do not have to have any skills specific to making the product other than good taste and clever marketing (and there's nothing wrong with that). There is also the issue of the methods and speed with which developing countries catch up with developed countries.

After World War II, a lot of jobs went to Japan from elsewhere. Japanese factories produced copied goods at low prices until their labour costs grew to equal those in the West. Then the jobs making those goods went elsewhere. Japanese factories eventually shifted to making high-quality products, and factories elsewhere now copy them. It took Japan thirty years to make the shift to no longer copying existing designs; it will take those elsewhere only three years now. Germany is now the number-one exporter of unique designs, but their products will be copied and produced at less cost for similar quality very soon, thanks to machines.

When Japan got into the act, the developed world had 500 million people involved in it, and Japan had 60 million people. Today's developed world has 1 billion people, and countries getting into the act – India, China, Indonesia, and some smaller countries – have a combined total of 2.5 billion people. It is unimaginable what effect today's advanced technology will have on the world economy. Many predictive models for future developments concentrate on only one change without considering all the other changes happening at the same time.

Goods and services produced by machines/ robots can easily satisfy the needs of an increased population, but the masses of this increased population will not find jobs if the present economic structure remains in place.

Advancements in technology, together with the number of people entering into the labour market, leave the future almost unpredictable, because the number of people involved in this system diminishes. That is, the number of people depending on the economic structure, rather than contributing to it, increases tremendously (and that *is* happening). Thus, the economic system in its present form will not generate sufficient money to support all the people in the world in the future.

Some activities have already been set aside from this economic system and moved into the charity system because they've been considered unaffordable.

However, if things need to be done, we should not have to say thank you for having them done. Instead, things that need to be done should be included within our economic structure, and we should be able to pay for them.

It is already an accepted opinion that the world is overpopulated. A similarly accepted opinion about numbers is that the number of A students in India is higher than the number of all students in the United States. These statistics will have an unpredictable effect on our future. History repeats itself but at a much faster pace.

Present efforts to prevent jobs from going to low-labour-cost countries or to robots can be compared with attempts to treat cancer with plasters.

To be absolutely correct, the issue is no longer simply one of labour going to lower-cost countries. The issue is much more complex due to technological developments, total population, and a much faster rate of catch-up compared to the past.

In the 1960s, my family had one bicycle, but an American family had two cars. Now, I don't have a tablet PC, but the sons of farmers in most developing countries do have them. Technology is spreading at a phenomenal rate. This shows that the difference between developed and developing countries is different from what it used to be.

Disappearing jobs are a fact of life in today's fast-developing world, and they have (and will have) a devastating effect on the way we live. So we'd better focus on how to deal with this issue proactively.

Some people may argue that besides nature and economics, government is also a major factor influencing human development. I disagree with this idea. Whatever the government, its perspective on labour is the same: it depends on affordability:

- Do we implement universal health care?

  o Government: We can't afford it.

- Do we go green?

  o Government: We can't afford it.

- Do we give retirees pensions?

  o Government: We can't afford it.

- Do we build high-speed trains?

  o Government: We can't afford it.

So we are back to only two primary influences on our lives: laws of economics, and laws of nature. The current consequences are much subtler than they were in the past.

The Arab Spring was not about the ruling regime; it was about jobs – or, more precisely, the lack of jobs – and about citizens having their backs against the wall. The population in the Middle East has exploded in the last thirty years, at 25 per cent each year, and there were no jobs to meet that increase in labour.

This "spring thing" started in Tunisia, North Africa: a university graduate who could not find a job had to resort to selling fruit, a business for which he had no license, and a government agent pushed him over the edge. He had no safety net, and being desperate, he killed himself publicly, setting himself on fire in front of the city hall. Many recognised that desperate act, and it led to a country-wide uprising, which then spread over the border into Egypt and then to other Middle East countries. The movement had little to do with government. Countries with less population density and smaller populations were affected less.

If you live outside the Middle East, do not think that your country is safe from a similar wave. Spain and Greece had a taste of uprising for one of the same reasons: no jobs. If a country has jobs or offers its people a safety net (e.g., unemployment benefits), a country's population is manageable.

Chapter 3

Analysis and Prediction

In our present economic system (which is man-made and *can* be changed), the number of paid jobs is diminishing. The ratio of unpaid people is increasing. In the present system, those who are paid somehow pay to support the unpaid people.

This is a matter of fact, and those with jobs cannot kill those without them or send them to another planet (a definite no-no!).

The paid people will increasingly resist having their spendable income go to support the unpaid.

This will ultimately lead to a two-grade society:

Grade 1 – the people who hold paid jobs

Grade 2 – the people who do not hold paid jobs

The people in grade two will be different from today's jobless people, who are mainly those with less education than others and who do not have a united voice although they are many. The new generation of well-educated but unpaid people will probably organise themselves better within our democratic system. They will form a powerful group with one objective.

Anarchy may very well be on the horizon. It flares up occasionally the moment the jobless perceive injustice. This results in an outbreak of self-service shopping without stopping at the cash register (looting) and rioting.

Another disturbing factor is that banks force themselves on us with never-ending advertising campaigns. Banks have no real purpose in our system, and they know that and so they spent so much money on advertising to convince us otherwise. They do not contribute to society but take a cut from every transaction that both paid people and unpaid people make. In 2013 a bank announced a multibillion-US-dollar profit in a newspaper while on the same page indicating that they were planning to reduce their workforce by three thousand jobs.

Charity also masks the present situation, although some states have attempted to calculate the economic volume of charity so that it can be included in economic analyses.

The present economic system should be changed, and changes should incorporate the latest technologies, for we've seen so much technological change, yet the political picture has not changed in two hundred years. The people in Great Britain decided two hundred years ago on the one-person, one-vote system, but they still hang on to the House of Lords, filled with people according to heredity. Those are contradictory ideas. Politicians seem to be more interested in re-election than in government. I don't blame them; I blame the system.

Government is supposed to lead us into the future, so why is it that most governments still live in the past? Even democratic systems are stuck in the past, with people elected to speak for those they govern for four years – when businesses adapt their plans quarterly!

If we want a sustainable future for ourselves, we need to act fast to make changes in tune with today's technology.

Chapter 4

Solution

I wish I could leave this chapter empty because I feel that, although I am reasonably good at analysing the present situation, it is so difficult to come up with a solution and proposal for a new system. However, many people believe that not proposing a solution disqualifies people from commenting on the problems of the present system.

In my defence, our present system has been built over hundreds of years, bit by bit by many very clever people. For one person to come up with a new system that solves all is a bit too much to ask.

Therefore, I will propose ideas for foundational elements for a new system, leaving the elements to be built upon that foundation to be derived from the collective input of all people.

I will not accept the opinion that the people do not know what they want! Such thinking is passé.

It is the duty of today's government to inform the people about the options, to listen to the people's opinions, and to act accordingly.

My message to governments is that people are not really as stupid as governments would like them to be.

We could organise a worldwide discussion after sharing educational information, which should not be confused with indoctrination or propaganda. Some of the smartest people could express their opinions and then let the masses decide.

Earlier in this book, I concluded that the laws of economics concentrate on developing businesses in hopes that people will benefit. Now I'll refine that statement: let us concentrate on *people*, and businesses will benefit.

The new system could consider paying people for their contributions to society instead of paying them only for their contributions to the economy. This new system should also take evolution into account, with evolution working similar to the way it works in nature – affecting all.

A system like that would allow a lot more people (if not all) to participate in the economic system.

In discussing this subject, I often ask, "Which people contribute to society tremendously and do not get paid for that contribution?" I have yet to get the right answer, but many reply, "Mothers." Without them, we wouldn't even be here. They spend their lives shaping the people on this planet.

Ignoring large portions of our society such as mothers will lead to anarchy sooner or later. Are we going to wait until that happens (and it will happen) and deal with it retroactively, or are we going to prove that we have learned from history and be proactive?

We are smarter now. And we are getting smarter faster.

Are we going to continue to be distracted by details such as emerging markets (Chinese, Indian, Indonesian, etc.) and robots who are taking our jobs, or are we going to prepare ourselves for the future? Let us try to design a system that follows natural processes, including evolution.

Our present system rewards individuals and corporations for their activities, and that is good, but it should be recognised that this individual or corporation would not get any reward without the rest of us. That means that we collectively contribute to this reward. Suppliers stick their necks out to make goods or provide services, but consumers stick their necks out too, to buy these products and services. The consumers are as much part of the system as the suppliers. We should try to find a system in which these cooperating groups mutually benefit from each other in a way that evolves.

Another feature of our present system is that the taxes skim off the rewards of individuals and corporations and redistribute that portion of rewards to others. This sounds fair, but the power of redistribution lies in the hands of a limited number of people elected to limited terms by a limited portion of the people.

The more you think about it, the more unjust you realise it is.

In the animal world, many predators, including killer whales, lions, and hyenas, have evolved to work together to survive. Although they are aggressive towards their prey, for the most part they live together in harmony. I do not wish to suggest that we learn from animals but I suggest that we learn from the way nature evolves living creatures in all aspects (develop social behaviour, adapt lifestyle to changes and equip bodies to meet environmental requirements).

Let us learn from that and come up with a system in which every human being has a value at birth and can arrange his or her own life. The person's value can then increase (or decrease) depending on his or her contributions to society.

The idea of contributions to society should be the cornerstone of the system's continued evolution, thus turning us away from our present destructive path.

Our society considers many things to be necessary that we cannot afford; therefore, some of these things are now done by volunteers and are supported by charity. Many people depend on this type of support, and these people should be grateful for it.

Such contributions benefit society.

Development happens in different ways and at different rates, and we all know that the levelling process cannot be stopped, so why fight it?

There is a longstanding fight between the conservative and the progressive viewpoints about accepting new things. The difference between having conservatives in control versus having progressives in control is typically a difference of fifteen years in when developments come about. Regardless, developments will happen, so trying to stop them or slow them down is counterproductive. For example, tram conductors disappeared long time ago, although people fought to keep tram-conducting jobs. Drivers are next.

Some advanced countries consider the advancement of other countries threatening. However, these other countries *will* advance. There is no stopping them, and any attempts to slow down the pace of advancement results only in unnecessary tension.

Evolution is a constant process. Let us learn from nature, put our heads together, and come up with a system that allows development to happen by evolution.

It is time that we learned how to live together by using one another's strengths to survive. Throughout history, nations have risen and fallen. This has often happened when one nation has overpowered other nations. Then other nations have grown stronger and caused the fall of the conquerors.

We humans do not accept being used or controlled by others. Most countries no longer have such overwhelming military dominance today, but as the ratio of the working people diminishes and the ratio of non-working people increases, working people develop dominance over non-working people. Ultimately, this imbalance will disrupt society.

We are on the way to self-destruction.

Besides our ability to communicate in writing, our use of money separates us from the rest of the animals. It is the way that we put money to (mis) use that ultimately leads to failure.

We invented paper money, which was originally only worth something if it was backed by a valuable resource such as gold. We have already done away with commodity currency and turned to fiat currency, which is a step in the right direction.

Let us find a way to make the next step. It will not be easy, but let us rise to the challenge.

The way our system uses money now divides people into those who have it and those who do not – those who can make it and those who cannot. Instead we should consider an economic system that values contributions to society, thus including all people.

The difficulty, I suppose, is how we determine the value of contributions to society and how we trade that value.

Considering all we've achieved so far, this should not be a very hard nut to crack.

The argument that it is not possible is not a valid excuse to keep us from trying. Many things which could not even be imagined in the past can now be done and even impact our daily lives. We can imagine this different approach, so it can be done.

The imbalance between developed and developing countries is probably the biggest obstacle. However, we have agreed on rules for human rights, which stipulate society's obligations to individuals. It is time to institute rules for human duties, which stipulate individuals' obligations to society.

Chapter 5

Conclusions

This chapter summarizes the statements made in the book:

- The laws of nature are indiscriminate.

- The world economy is man-made.

- We can change the way we have organised the world economy.

- The world economy can be made more in tune with today's technology such that it includes all people – and in such a way that the world society evolves.

- Nature has an evolutionary concept, and societies were kind of ideal when mankind started. We lived in small communities in which older members led us. The communities grew bigger, and countries were formed lead by leaders with ultimate power. Many leaders no longer have this ultimate power, and we are moving to a society with more individual rights and freedom. We seem, however, to have taken a wrong turn when money was selected as the main driving force in our lives, as that money can only be made through the commercial circuit. Having said that, money may have been the stepping stone to lead us to where we are now.

- We may want to say goodbye to the present form of money and replace it with something that is not dependent on commercial business only.

- We could look into a new system that rewards contribution to *society*.

- That concept should both reward individual efforts and consider our basic human features of greed and envy.

- The banks have a limited function. They seem to add little or nothing to society, but they take a portion of all transactions.

- Individual freedoms and rights granted by society should be linked to individual duties to society.

Printed in the United States
By Bookmasters